The following pronunciations are very simplified and a basic introduction to **Lakota language**. In the Lakota language, these are the numbers from one to ten:

1. **Wanji** (wahn-zhee)

2. **Numpa** (noom-pah)

3. **Yamni** (yah-muh-nee)

4. **Topa** (doe-pah)

5. **Zaptan** (zah-puh-tahn { a soft "N" up in your nose, not a hard "N"})

6. **Šakpe** (shock-pay)

7. **Šakowin** (shah-koe-ween)

8. **Šagloġan** (shah-guh-low-gahn { hard "G" on the last syllable as in "gum" while you have a little bit of chocolate in your mouth})

9. **Napčiunka** (nahp-chee-oon-kah)

10. **Wikčemna** (week-chehm-uh-nah)

imagineIF Libraries
Kalispell Montana

TATANKA COUNTS

ISBN: 978-1987668575

MY NAME IS TATANKA, THE LAKOTA (SIOUX) WORD FOR "BUFFALO".

I LIVE IN SOUTH DAKOTA.

LET'S COUNT SOME THINGS THAT I SEE IN SOUTH DAKOTA.

ONE EAGLE

WAMBLI WANJI

TWO CROWS

KANĠI NUMPA

THREE MEADOWLARKS

THAŠIYAGMUNKA YAMNI

FOUR COYOTES

ṠUNKMANITU TOPA

FIVE CROCUSES

HOKŠIČEKPA WAHČA ZAPTAN

SIX HORSES

ŠUNKAWAKAN ŠAKPE

SEVEN DEER

TAȞČA ŠAKOWIN

EIGHT PINE TREES

WAZI ŠAGLOĠAN

NINE RABBITS

MASTINĊA NAPĊIUNKA

TEN BUFFALO

TATANKA WIKĊEMNA

VERY GOOD! (LILA WAŚTE!)

THANK YOU (PILAMAYA, OR PILAMAYAYE FOR MALES) FOR COUNTING WITH ME!

SEE YOU LATER! (TOKŚA!)

These are the Lakota words for the things we counted:

Eagle: wambli (WAHM-buh-LEE)

Crow: kanǧi (kahn-GHEE { a hard "g" with chocolate in your mouth})

Meadowlark: Thašiyagmunka (tah-SHEE-yah-gah-moon-kah)

Rabbit: mastinča (mahs-TEEN-chah)

Coyote: šunkmanitu (shoonk-MAHN-ee-too)

Crocus: hokšičekpa wahča (HOEK-she-CHECK-pah walk-CHAH
{ not really a "K", more like a hard "H" with chocolate in your mouth})

Horse: šunkawakan (SHOONK-ah-wah-KAHN, also
sunkakan=SHOON-kah-kahn with a soft "N" up in your nose)

Deer: tahča (TALK-chah { not really a "k" at the end of the first syllable,
more like a hard "h" with chocolate in your mouth})

Pine tree: wazi (wah-ZEE)

Buffalo: tatanka (tah-TAHNK-ah, also dah-DAHN-kah)
Some people pronounce "T" on the front of a word as a "D".

Very good!: Lila wašte! (LEE-lah wahsh-TAY)

Thank you: pilamaya (pea-LAH-mah-yah). If a male is talking,
add ye (yeh) or yelo (yeh-low) after pilamaya.

See you later!: Tokša! (DOKE-shah)

ABOUT THE AUTHOR

Melissa Two Crow was raised in the Black Hills of South Dakota. She has a B.S. in Elementary Education with Minors in Spanish and American Indian Studies, a Master of Science in Curriculum and Instruction, a B.S. in American Indian Studies with a Minor in Teaching English to Speakers of Other Languages, and a B.A. in East Asian Studies.

Melissa taught preschool through adult learning classes for about forty years and was a seasonal interpreter of Lakota (Sioux) culture for seven years. Melissa started writing at a very young age when she wrote her own versions of Dr. Seuss poems on the inside covers of her books. Then she moved on to writing greeting cards, complete with "trademarks" on the back, for every family occasion.

She has wanted to be a professional writer ever since her fourth-grade teacher wanted to keep a poem Melissa wrote for class. She wrote for the school newspaper all through Junior High and High School and was a member of Quill and Scroll. Melissa has a grown son who is a member of the U.S. Army. He has a lovely wife and three beautiful children. They all love books as much as she does.

MORE FROM JASON EAGLESPEAKER

COLLECT 'EM ALL !!!

AUTHENTICALLY INDIGENOUS NAPI STORIES:
Napi and the Rock
Napi and the Bullberries
Napi and the Wolves
Napi and the Buffalo
Napi and the Chickadees
Napi and the Coyote
Napi and the Elk
Napi and the Gophers
Napi and the Mice
Napi and the Prairie Chickens
Napi and the Bobcat
... and many more Napi tales to come

AUTHENTICALLY INDIGENOUS GRAPHIC NOVELS:
UNeducation: A Residential School Graphic Novel
Napi the Trixster: A Blackfoot Graphic Novel
UNeducation, Vol 2

AUTHENTICALLY INDIGENOUS COLORING BOOKS:
Napi: A Coloring Experience
UNeducation: A Coloring Experience
Completely Capricious Coloring Collection
A Day at the Powwow (grayscale coloring)

AUTHENTICALLY INDIGENOUS KIDS BOOKS:
Teeias Goes to a Powwow (a series)

ANOTHER WWW.EAGLESPEAKER.COM PROJECT

WWW.EAGLESPEAKER.COM

**IF YOU ABSOLUTELY LOVED THIS BOOK (OR EVEN JUST KIND OF LIKED IT), PLEASE FIND IT ON AMAZON.COM AND LEAVE A QUICK REVIEW. YOUR WORDS HELP MORE THAN YOU MAY REALIZE.

CPSIA information can be obtained
at www.ICGtesting.com
Printed in the USA
LVHW072248210819
628539LV00019B/527/P

* 9 7 8 1 9 8 7 6 6 8 5 7 5 *